The FUNNIEST Riddle Book EVER!

What do elephants have that
no other animals have?

Baby elephants.

by
Joseph Rosenbloom

illustrations by
Hans Wilhelm

S **Sterling Publishing Co., Inc.** **New York**

Text copyright © 1985 by Joseph Rosenbloom
Illustrations copyright © 1985 by Hans Wilhelm, Inc.
Published by Sterling Publishing Co., Inc.
Two Park Avenue, New York, N.Y. 10016
Distributed in Australia by Oak Tree Press Co., Ltd.
P.O. Box K514 Haymarket, Sydney 2000, N.S.W.
Distributed in the United Kingdom by Blandford Press
Link House, West Street, Poole, Dorset BH15 1LL, England
Distributed in Canada by Oak Tree Press, Ltd.
% Canadian Manda Group, P.O. Box 920, Station U
Toronto, Ontario M8Z 5P9
Manufactured in the United States of America

Library of Congress Cataloging in Publication Data

Rosenbloom, Joseph.
 The funniest riddle book ever!

 Ages 5-8
 Summary: An illustrated collection of humorous riddles.
 1. Riddles, Juvenile. [1. Riddles, 2. Jokes]
I. Wilhelm, Hans, 1945– , ill. II. Title.
PN6371.5.R6116 1984   818′.5402   84-16192
 ISBN 0-8069-4698-9
 ISBN 0-8069-4699-7 (lib. bdg.)

How could twelve children and two dogs be under an umbrella, and not get wet?

Because it wasn't raining.

How do you know that carrots are good for the eyes?

Have you ever seen a rabbit wearing eyeglasses?

Why do flies walk on ceilings?

If they walked on the floor, someone might step on them.

What is small, purple and dangerous?

A grape with a six-shooter.

Why do witches fly on broomsticks?
It's better than walking.

Where does an 800-pound gorilla sleep?
Anywhere it wants.

What rises in the morning
and waves all day?
A flag.

What is black and white and red all
over?
A sunburned zebra.

What is big and white
and is found on the Equator?

A lost polar bear.

What did the boy octopus
say to the girl octopus?

*"I want to hold your hand,
hand, hand, hand, hand,
hand, hand, hand. . . ."*

Why do lions eat raw meat?
*Because they don't know
how to cook.*

How do you get a mouse to fly?
Buy it an airline ticket.

What is white outside, green inside, and hops?

A frog sandwich.

How can you tell
there's an elephant in the refrigerator?

The door won't shut.

What should you say when you meet a monster with two heads?

"Hello, hello!"

What time is it when a monster sits on a chair?

Time to get a new chair.

What do you do when a monster sneezes?

Get out of the way!

How do you talk to giants?

Use BIG WORDS!

What is black and yellow and goes "Zzub zzub?

A bee going backwards.

What is a grasshopper?

An insect on a pogo stick.

Why do postmen carry letters?

Because the letters can't carry themselves.

Why do firemen wear red suspenders?

To keep their pants up.

What did the big chimney say to the little chimney?

"You smoke too much."

What has two wheels, two horns and gives milk?

A cow on a motorcycle.

Why do monkeys
scratch themselves?

*Because they're the
only ones who
know where it
itches.*

Why is an elephant
large, gray and lumpy?

*Because if it were
small, white and
smooth, it would be
an aspirin.*

Why does a giraffe have a long neck?

Because its head is so far from its body.

What is the difference between a mailbox and a kangaroo?

If you don't know, I won't send you out to mail a letter.

What does a 200-pound
mouse say?

"Here, kitty, kitty!"

What sound do two
porcupines make
when they kiss?

"Ouch!"

What did one flea say to the other flea?

"Shall we walk or shall we take a dog?"

What is the strongest animal in the world?

A turtle, because it carries its house on its back.

What has a hump and sings like a bird?

A camel carrying a canary.

What makes more noise than one squealing pig?

Two squealing pigs.

What do you do with a pickle when it is one year old?

Wish it a happy birthday.

What is yellow and swims underwater?

A yellow submarine.

What goes "Clump, clump, clump, swish?"

An elephant with a wet sneaker.